TABLE OF CONTENTS

CHAPTER 1

Parts of a Map 4

CHAPTER 2

Borders and Colors 10

CHAPTER 3

Using Political Maps 18

QUICK FACTS & TOOLS

Map Quiz 22

Glossary 23

Index 24

To Learn More 24

CHAPTER 1

PARTS OF A MAP

A map is a drawing of an area and its features. Maps show us where places are.

LET'S READ MAPS!

POLITICAL MAPS

by Adrianne Velasco

pogo

Ideas for Parents and Teachers

Pogo Books let children practice reading informational text while introducing them to nonfiction features such as headings, labels, sidebars, maps, and diagrams, as well as a table of contents, glossary, and index.

Carefully leveled text with a strong photo match offers early fluent readers the support they need to succeed.

Before Reading

- "Walk" through the book and point out the various nonfiction features. Ask the student what purpose each feature serves.
- Look at the glossary together. Read and discuss the words.

During Reading

- Have the child read the book independently.
- Invite them to list questions that arise from reading.

After Reading

- Discuss the child's questions. Talk about how they might find answers to those questions.
- Prompt the child to think more. Ask: What continent do you live on? Can you find where you live on a political map?

Pogo Books are published by Jump!
3500 American Blvd W, Suite 150
Bloomington, MN 55431
www.jumplibrary.com

Jump! is a division of FlutterBee Education Group.

Library of Congress Cataloging-in-Publication Data

Names: Velasco, Adrianne, author.
Title: Political maps / by Adrianne Velasco.
Description: Minneapolis, MN: Jump!, Inc., 2026.
Series: Let's read maps!
Audience: Ages 7-10
Identifiers: LCCN 2024058900 (print)
LCCN 2024058901 (ebook)
ISBN 9798892139274 (hardcover)
ISBN 9798892139281 (paperback)
ISBN 9798892139298 (ebook)
Subjects: LCSH: Maps–Political aspects–Juvenile literature. | Map reading–Juvenile literature.
Classification: LCC GA130 .V453 2026 (print)
LCC GA130 (ebook)
DDC 912.01/4–dc23/eng/20250111
LC record available at https://lccn.loc.gov/2024058900
LC ebook record available at https://lccn.loc.gov/2024058901

Editor: Jenna Gleisner
Designer: Emma Almgren-Bersie

Photo Credits: PorcupenWorks/Shutterstock, cover, 14; gio_banfi/iStock, 1; switchpipipi/iStock, 3; iofoto/iStock, 4; Peter Hermes Furian/Shutterstock, 5, 8-9, 10, 18; dikobraziy/iStock, 6-7; brichuas/Shutterstock, 11 (map), 12-13; Foxberry/Shutterstock, 11 (background); soulcld/iStock, 13, 14-15; Bardocz Peter/Shutterstock, 16-17; Rawpixel/Shutterstock, 19; Chachawal Prapai/iStock, 20-21; Cartarium/iStock, 22; hyotographics/Shutterstock, 23.

Printed in the United States of America at Corporate Graphics in North Mankato, Minnesota.

Maps have tools to help us read them. A map key tells us what **symbols** on a map mean. A red line could stand for a major road. Dots stand for cities. Stars stand for **capitals**.

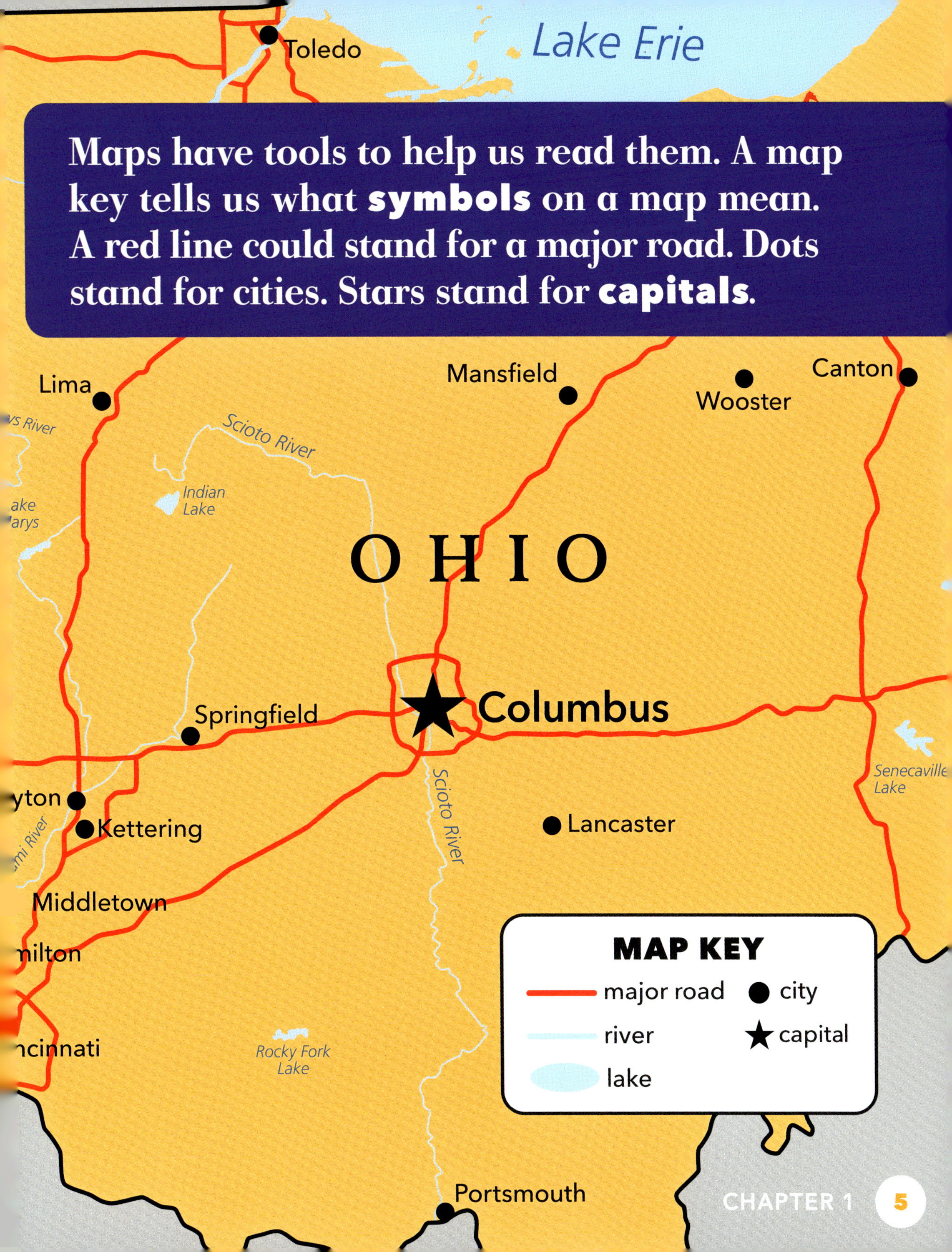

ARCTIC OCEAN
Greenland
UNITED STATES
Beaufort Sea
Kaujuitog (Resolute)
Baffin Bay
Inuvik
Dawson City
YUKON TERRITORY
Whitehorse
Watson Lake
Cambridge Bay
Echo Bay
NORTHWEST TERRITORIES
Yellowknife
Iqaluit
Fort Nelson
Hay River
Fort Smith
Ivujivik
NUNAVUT
BRITISH COLUMBIA
Prince George
ALBERTA
SASKATCHEWAN
Edmonton
Flin Flon
MANITOBA
Hudson Bay
Chisasibi
Victoria
Vancouver
Calgary
Saskatoon
Lethbridge
Regina
Moosonee
ONTARIO
Winnipeg
Thunder Bay
UNITED STATES
Sudbury
Ottawa
Toronto
Hamilton
London
Windsor
latitude line
longitude line

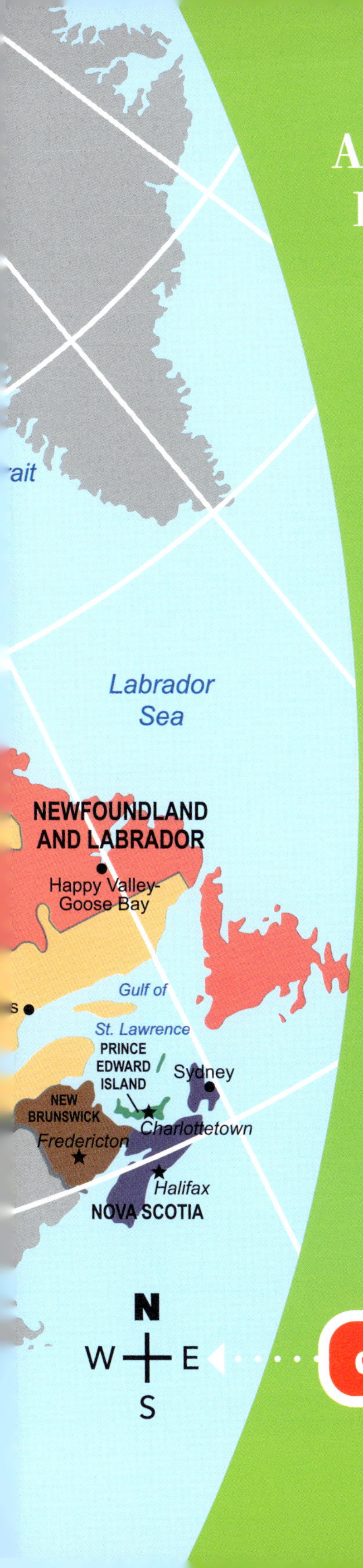

compass rose

A compass rose has four points. Each shows a direction. They are north (N), east (E), south (S), and west (W).

Latitude lines and **longitude lines** are imaginary. They cross Earth on a map. They make a **grid**. We can use them to find exact **locations**.

WHAT DO YOU THINK?

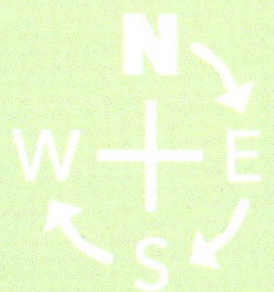

The saying "**N**ever **E**at **S**oggy **W**affles" can remind us of the order of directions! Start at north. Go to the right, around the circle. Read the saying. What other sayings could work to remember the directions?

Maps are small drawings of larger places. A scale tells us how large an area or **distance** is. One inch (2.5 centimeters) on a map could be three miles (4.8 kilometers) in real life.

SCALE
1 inch (2.5 cm) = 3 miles (4.8 km)
New Rochelle
Clifton
New Jersey
Hudson River
New York
Jersey City
ewark
New York City
Atlantic Ocean
N
W
E
S

CHAPTER 2

BORDERS AND COLORS

Political maps show the names and locations of places.

Some political maps show the whole world. These maps show the seven **continents**. Each is shown in a different color. Why? It helps us tell them apart.

Borders show us where one continent or country ends. They show us where another begins. We can see what countries are on each continent. We can see what countries are next to one another.

TAKE A LOOK!

Political maps show what countries share borders. For example, Canada and the United States share a border. Take a look!

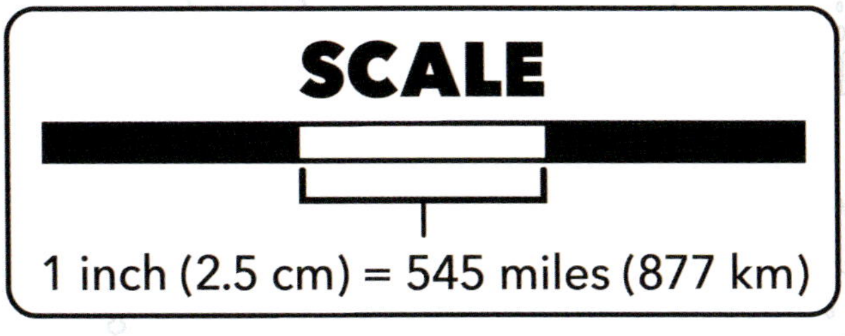

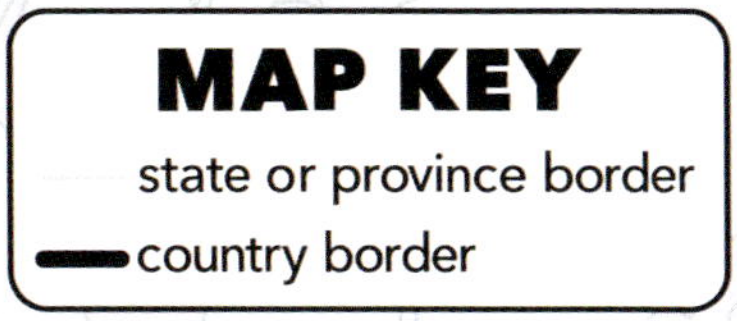

Some political maps show just one country. Borders show which states are next to one another. They show how big each state is.

WHAT DO YOU THINK?

Borders tell governments what land they own and are in charge of. Do you think clear borders are important? Why or why not?

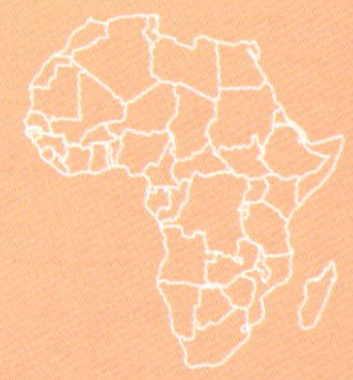

New Hampshire
Maine
Vermont
Montana
North Dakota
Minnesota
Massachusetts
New York
Rhode Island
Wisconsin
Michigan
Connecticut
South Dakota
Pennsylvania
New Jersey
Wyoming
Washington D.C.
Delaware
Iowa
Ohio
Maryland
Nebraska
Illinois
Indiana
West Virginia
Virginia
Colorado
Kansas
Kentucky
Missouri
North Carolina
Tennessee
South Carolina
Oklahoma
Arkansas
New Mexico
Alabama
Georgia
Mississippi
Texas
Louisiana
Florida
N
W
E
S

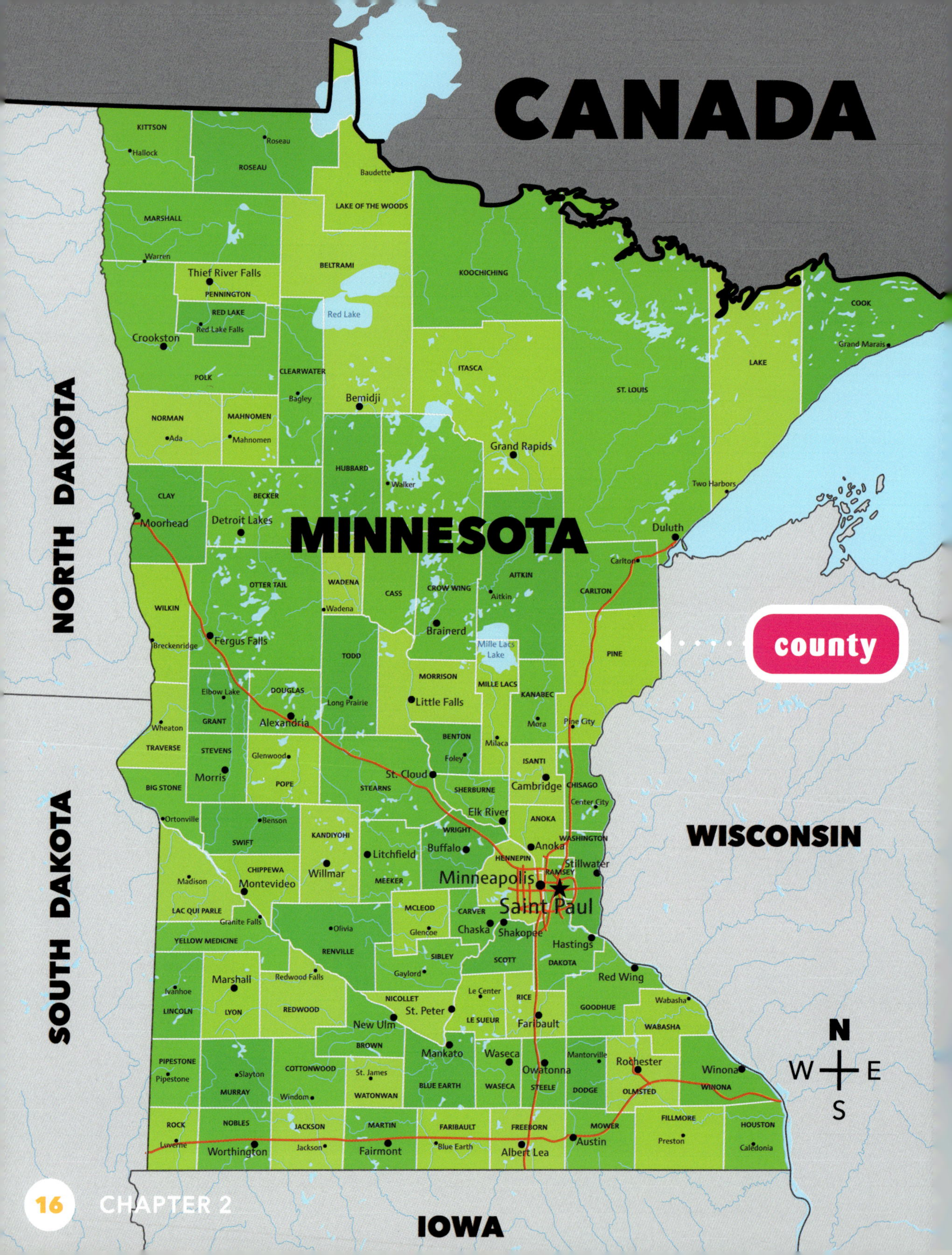
CANADA
MINNESOTA
NORTH DAKOTA
SOUTH DAKOTA
WISCONSIN
IOWA
county
N
W
E
S
KITTSON
Hallock
Roseau
ROSEAU
Baudette
LAKE OF THE WOODS
MARSHALL
Warren
BELTRAMI
KOOCHICHING
Thief River Falls
PENNINGTON
RED LAKE
Red Lake Falls
Red Lake
Crookston
POLK
CLEARWATER
Bagley
Bemidji
ITASCA
ST. LOUIS
LAKE
COOK
Grand Marais
NORMAN
Ada
MAHNOMEN
Mahnomen
Grand Rapids
HUBBARD
Walker
Two Harbors
CLAY
Moorhead
BECKER
Detroit Lakes
Duluth
Carlton
OTTER TAIL
WADENA
Wadena
CASS
CROW WING
AITKIN
Aitkin
CARLTON
WILKIN
Breckenridge
Fergus Falls
Brainerd
Mille Lacs Lake
PINE
TODD
MORRISON
MILLE LACS
KANABEC
Elbow Lake
DOUGLAS
Long Prairie
Little Falls
Mora
Pine City
Wheaton
GRANT
Alexandria
BENTON
Milaca
TRAVERSE
STEVENS
Glenwood
Foley
ISANTI
Morris
POPE
St. Cloud
Cambridge
CHISAGO
BIG STONE
STEARNS
SHERBURNE
Center City
Ortonville
Benson
Elk River
ANOKA
WRIGHT
SWIFT
KANDIYOHI
Buffalo
Anoka
WASHINGTON
HENNEPIN
Stillwater
CHIPPEWA
Litchfield
RAMSEY
Madison
Montevideo
Willmar
MEEKER
Minneapolis
Saint Paul
LAC QUI PARLE
MCLEOD
CARVER
Granite Falls
Chaska
Shakopee
Olivia
Glencoe
YELLOW MEDICINE
RENVILLE
Hastings
SIBLEY
SCOTT
DAKOTA
Gaylord
Red Wing
Redwood Falls
Marshall
Ivanhoe
Le Center
NICOLLET
RICE
Wabasha
LINCOLN
LYON
REDWOOD
St. Peter
GOODHUE
LE SUEUR
New Ulm
Faribault
WABASHA
BROWN
PIPESTONE
Mankato
Waseca
Mantorville
Rochester
Pipestone
Slayton
COTTONWOOD
St. James
Owatonna
Winona
MURRAY
WASECA
STEELE
DODGE
WINONA
Windom
WATONWAN
BLUE EARTH
OLMSTED
FILLMORE
ROCK
NOBLES
JACKSON
MARTIN
FARIBAULT
FREEBORN
MOWER
HOUSTON
Luverne
Worthington
Jackson
Fairmont
Blue Earth
Albert Lea
Austin
Preston
Caledonia

Other political maps focus on smaller areas. A political map of a state shows **county** borders. It shows major roads. It also shows a state's towns and cities. Bigger towns and cities are often bigger on a map. Small towns look smaller.

DID YOU KNOW?

Political maps can include features like rivers and lakes.

CHAPTER 3

USING POLITICAL MAPS

Political maps are one of the most popular types of maps. Why? They make finding and checking information easy. Do you want to find the capital of Japan? Check a political map!

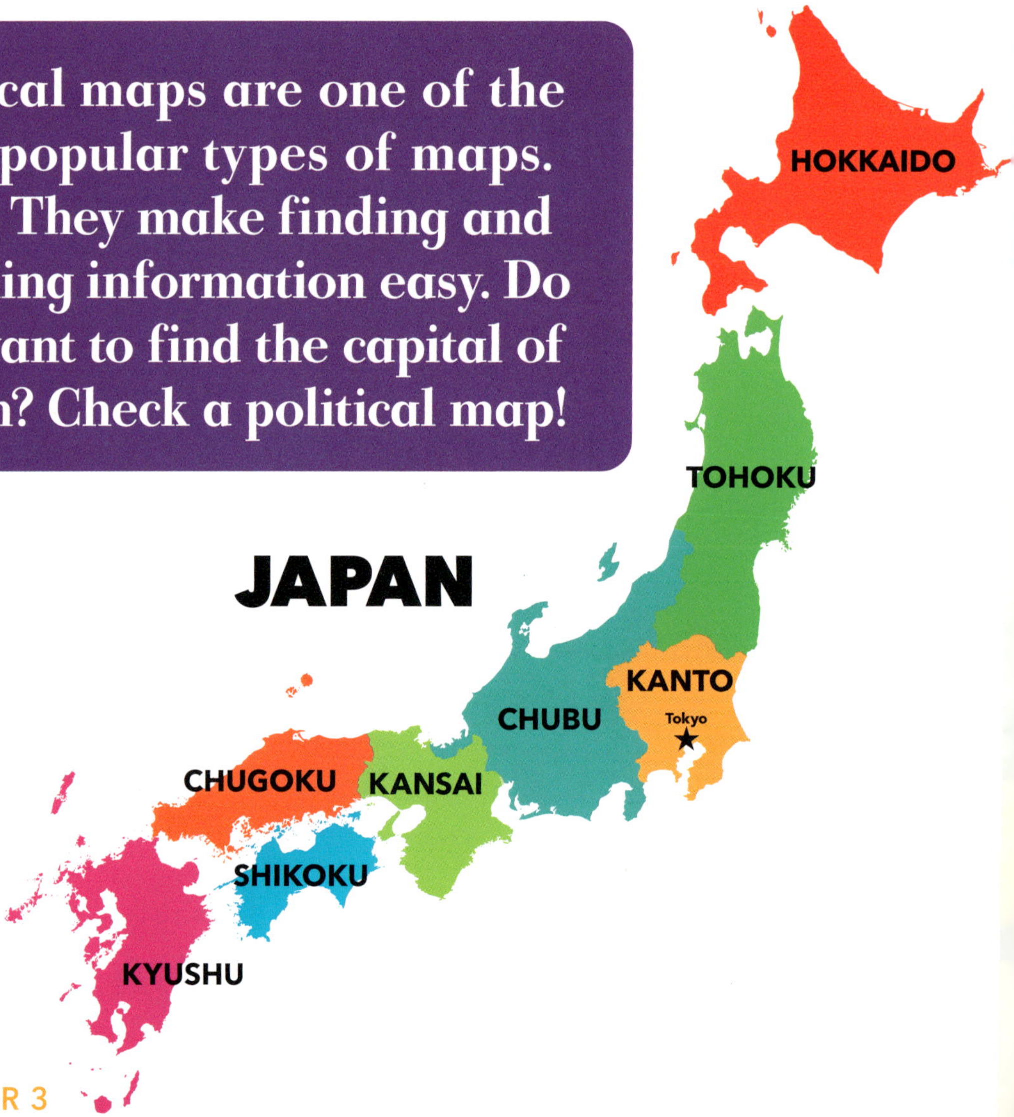

We use political maps to plan travel. Governments and schools use them, too. You might have a political map in your classroom!

Political maps tell us a lot about the world. They show the shapes and sizes of places. They show us continents and countries. They show us how places are connected. We can use them to find capitals and cities.

How do you use political maps?

QUICK FACTS & TOOLS

MAP QUIZ

Political maps show us borders, states, cities, and more. Use this map of Europe to answer the questions below!

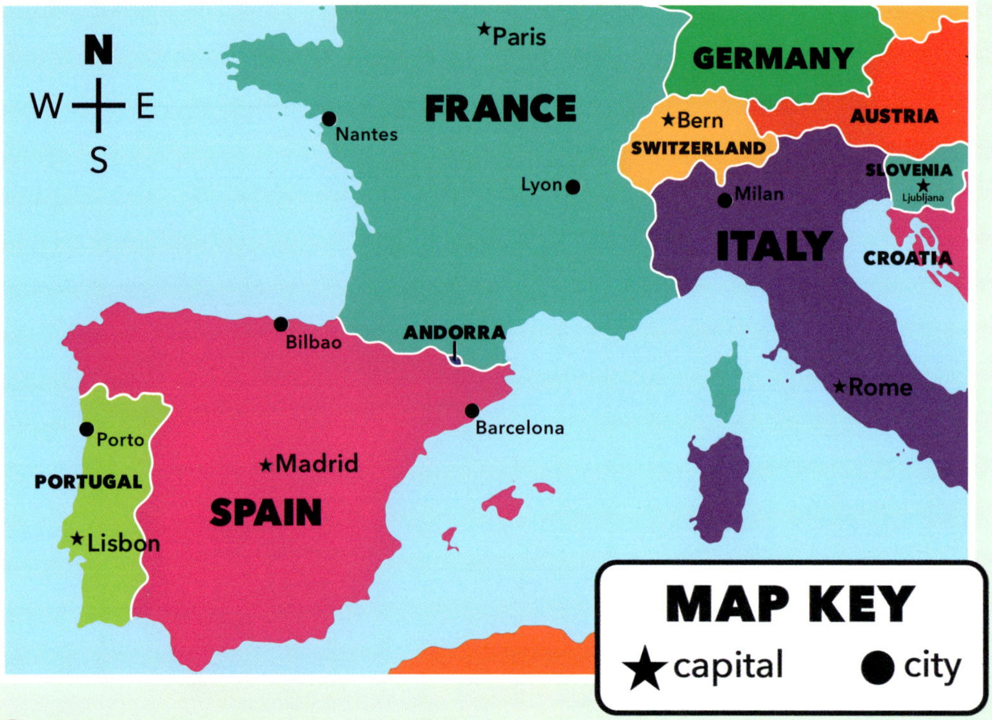

1. **What is the capital of Spain?**
2. **What country borders Portugal?**
3. **What country is west of Switzerland?**

Answer Key: 1) Madrid. 2) Spain. 3) France.

GLOSSARY

borders: Dividing lines between countries or regions.

capitals: The cities in states or countries where the government is based.

continents: The seven large landmasses of Earth. They are Asia, Africa, Europe, North America, South America, Australia, and Antarctica.

county: A division of a state with its own local government.

distance: The space between two places.

features: Particular parts of something.

grid: A network of evenly spaced vertical and horizontal lines that forms a regular pattern of squares.

latitude lines: Imaginary lines that circle Earth and run east to west. They measure distance north and south.

locations: Places or positions.

longitude lines: Imaginary lines that circle Earth and run north to south. They measure distance east and west.

symbols: Designs or objects that stand for something else.

INDEX

borders 12, 13, 14, 17
capitals 5, 18, 21
cities 5, 17, 21
color 11
compass rose 7
continents 11, 12, 21
country 12, 13, 14, 21
county 17
directions 7
distance 8
features 4, 17
governments 14, 19
grid 7
latitude lines 7
locations 7, 10
longitude lines 7
map key 5
names 10
road 5, 17
scale 8
states 14, 17
symbols 5
towns 17
world 11, 21

TO LEARN MORE

Finding more information is as easy as 1, 2, 3.

1. Go to www.factsurfer.com
2. Enter "politicalmaps" into the search box.
3. Choose your book to see a list of websites.

FACT SURFER